Unlearn Moderation:
Mindfood for Heretics

Krista Ann Hammerbacher Haapala

Unlearn Moderation: Mindford for Heretics

by

Krista Ann Hammerbacher Haapala

For more information on *Unlearn Moderation* or to book an event, visit kristahaapala.com.

Designed by David B. Grelck

Published internationally by 39 Revolutions Press

Printed in the United States

1 3 5 7 9 10 8 6 4 2

First Printing: June, 2015

ISBN: 978-1511997416

39 Revolutions Press

table of contents

I. think

II. seize

III. entwine

Foreword

I adore Krista. I mean, how could one not?

She's asked me many times for my opinions on her poetry, for critiques, perhaps knowing that once upon a time I was a hack performance poet in high school. So, you know, qualified. My poems even rhymed. It was how I rolled.

I find it so difficult to critique poetry, though, to even talk about it. Whenever I attempt, it feels as artificial as when I attempt to really talk about wine. I find myself using artifice, language that ultimately means nothing. And at the end, I instead only tell her "This is a poem. I found it to be good." Or something equally as non-poetic.

I think the reason that it's so hard is because poetry so artfully brings out feelings. In very minimal words, it can evoke the full spectrum of human emotion. When asked to quantify it somehow, I feel that any words I say may be reductionist, and sell the work short. When it certainly evokes deep feelings.

But I can speak to the woman. She, I tell you, she is something truly special. An original creation, never meant for mass production. Too great for that. She embodies the phrase lust for life, sucking the marrow from its bones. Her strength and passion makes me weak in the knees.

Krista and I share the uncanny habit of picking up projects the way most people pick up new TV series to watch. (I do that too.) An endless stack of things we ought to be doing in front of us, because how will it ever get finished unless we finish it. Sometimes it's hard to finish. Sometimes it's hard because we don't know what the other side of birthing looks like.

I am thrilled to be able to help midwife this project into the world. Because you need to read it. Her poetry is beautiful and complex and funny and moving. And other words that I won't say lest I start to sound like a pretentious prat. Because what her poetry, and she, means to me doesn't matter nearly as much as what it/she will mean to you.

And that's the beauty of the art, isn't it? That it can mean incredibly different things to different people. That you will see things completely different than I. The feelings and words it conjures in you will have your special direct connection to the work. Something pure and personal.

But there can be one thing in life with no doubt. That the goddess that is named Krista Ann Hammerbacher Haapala is unparalleled. To be able to catch a glimpse of her undeniably sexy brain is a privilege, and one we all would do well to savor. Like that fine wine.

And poetry.

Whereas I took five hundred words to say something about how I'll likely say nothing, it's because we're better at savoring when our mouths are closed, aren't we. When we're not talking about the wine or poetry or steak or ice cream. But just letting it fill us with texture and flavor.

And warmth.

And beauty.

And love.

~ David B. Grelck

for Bri

her·e·tic

/ˈherəˌtik/

noun

a human believing in or practicing religious heresy.

a human holding an opinion at odds with what is generally accepted.

synonyms: dissenter, nonconformist, freethinker, iconoclast

antonyms: conformist

Introduction

Our culture sings us the lullaby that we need to take things one step at a time. Behave. Eat your peas and you'll get dessert.

The reason we hear that message most is many humans find comfort in the rules, so it is stories of the rules that we hear. They speak from their limited experience, extolling moderation despite lack of evidence of its efficacy. The rule worshippers continue to eat their peas counting on the assumption that dessert awaits.

Yet there are those who feel the need to create. Creators will not be contained. The rules leave no room for innovation. So desperate to be an artist, to indulge in the sweetness of life, the creators leave the peas for the rule worshippers. Taking the risk to unlearn moderation, the creators become heretics and gorge themselves on dessert.

Heretics recognize that the balance to moderation is excess: excess compassion, excess peace, excess intensity. Every creator becomes a heretic by stepping outside the rules, even if just for a moment, to taste the sweetness of too much love for the world.

It is counterculture to risk connecting with the humans around us. Heretics embrace the suffering that comes from feeling too much. We have no time for moderation. Every breath is yours and ours together.

You are a creator. Don't be fooled. Words are art. Actions are art. You are an artist every day when you tell your child he's beautiful, when you say please and thank you, when you smile and hold the door for a stranger, when you take a photo of the sunset and post it for the world to see.

Every choice you make shapes the world.

You are a creator.

This mindfood is for you, my dear heretic. May you be sustained.

Why Poetry?

All words are emotion when we allow ourselves to be vulnerable, yet that is rare. Small talk is called small talk for a reason. No one is willing to open up and play big. So we dither in the weather and the pleasantries.

Poetry rejects pretense. Poetry is nakedness and nerves, love and death, bravery and simply breath. You really have to want it. And many of us cling to our numbness, at least occasionally. We can live numb in this world if we choose it.

Our culture enables us in our numbness. Listicles and easy likes take less than a second, hardly the time to even register true feeling.

Poetry asks us to commit, hold our breath for a bit to dive under. Truly sinking into the depths of emotion is always a risk. It is a risk we are less and less likely to take when we can be rewarded with the pellet of the follower and the like.

We are being sold interaction as connection and it is just not the same.

Why poetry? Because you are worthy of taking the risk. Your emotion is your lifeblood. You deserve to live awake.

Allow these words, any words, to foster emotion and cultivate connection. The world is richer than the advertisements let on. Be heretical. Be real.

~kahh

1.1.2015

Too loud. Too fast
They stand aghast
Too right. Too wrong
I shied from strong
Too much thinking. Too
confused.
I refuse to stand
accused of denying
my frenzied muse.
She courted me
I turned away
Yet openly she
chose to stay.
Her persistence seduced
me despite the
constant guarantee
of judgment that
I am too intense.
She willingly came to
my defense, so I
feel the draw of
recompense. As I
learned her, I
embraced the
wildness of her lack
of grace. She taught
me just how I
must live. All
who malign, I forgive.
Such is the price
of the creative

1. think

edges

Walk
through
shattered
rules
at your
own
risk.
The shards
are sharp,
with edges
of demons
of those
who oppose.

found

Your need
to search
will overcome
your belief
it will
never be
found.

When the discovery is made
even you will be surprised.

secret

Polite was years ago.
You missed her.
I buried her
under the
Temple of Indulgence.

(Now remember
that is our little secret.)

Polite was
such a
shrinking violet
anyway,
I am amused
she is
pushing up posies.

Indulgence?
Now, she is a handful.
Made me
build that temple...
always demanding,
then my capitulation.
When she
reaches out
and strokes
your cheek,
the electricity
intoxicates.

I do her bidding in
the trance
of knowing
I am ever standing
over
my grave.

And since
I buried Polite alive,
I obey when
Indulgence requires
me
to dance
It is her temple after
all.

heretical

Rising in me
from the shadow
I groom
is a heretical prominentia
destined to bloom.

The pressure
with breath
is gravity awry,
the compelling
is rabid
until I comply.

As pleasing
Cleopatra
was a fiery risk
worth swallowing death
just to be kissed,
I raise my hands
to the welcome
the flames
for burning just
as the prominentia
proclaims.

prime

Bend.
Pretend.
Your youth
will extend
deep into time
when you comprehend
that your mind sublime
smiles when you
accept every day
as your prime.
Seeking ecstasy
elsewhere than
where you are
is precisely when
all the pleasure fades
for you again.
Stake your claim,
you selfish soul,
if living awake is
indeed your goal.
Denying passion
takes a toll that,
without a doubt,
leaves you
less than whole.
Shine bright!
Grab all the stars
you can.
Unleash that
wicked master plan.

paperweight

You are
in every driver's seat
cursing the gridlock.

Think.

But alas,
that mass of
synaptic mess
just weighs you down.

The paperweight brain
is a choice.

The breeze blows through,
yet the archaic notions
and unthinking thoughts
stay safely pinned to the desk.

oppression

Where there is
smoke and mirrors,
there is
fire and denial.
Warm until it gets too hot.
Comforting until it is not.
The reflection morphing,
writhing with incongruence
between truth
and cultural lockstep
influence.
In that fire
choose to burn
that which in you
will not learn
that judgment is
the thief of essence
robbing all
of the unique luminescence
that lights the world
when purely reflected.

Let it be
oppression
rejected.

row

You won't see the need.
You'll feel it first.

That treadmill of monotony
will force your escape.

A refugee
from expectation
and guilt,
you build a boat
and carve an oar
from pure freedom
over years of confinement
by nothing but
your own conception
of the acceptable.

Your shoulders ache,
every stroke
putting distance
between you
and your antiquated
intention of the correct.

With a glimpse of absolution,
you row with renewed intention.

Your island beckons,
awaiting your
efflorescence
and ready to
champion your
tabula rasa.

right

What else can you do
beyond these words?
Deciphering symbols
shaped like
the chaos of the storm
in your mind.
Hearing the cadence
of the incessant
broadcast as
the voice of truth
to those who
will eat saccharin hope
with a spoon.
Context.
Respecting to some
seeing is believing.
Despite inhaling
the caustic irrationality,
they will choose
to gasp through
numbered breaths
to whisper
who is right.

charmed

Terror's answer
is not mine.
We all seek
the same
in time.

Pretending puzzles
feel the flow.
Instinct rules
it is not to know.

Hand to wall,
walk,
count the steps.
Dimensions emerge,
measuring, complex.

A trip so charmed
saves you while
landing then
in ropes defiled.

Listen now,
the sound of death
grows ever closer
with his breath.

Escape so hungry,
next red-hot.

Burning.

Falling.

Fear.

Caught.

Life's clamoring
shadows
do reach out.

Make each choice.
Force their doubt.

manufactured

The answer tickles,
plays at the edges
only ever partially
in the frame.

...this corner now...
...that side then...

Collecting the appearances,
piecing them together
like a conspiracy theorist
in a windowless,
underground
office.

The obsession,
the urgency of it.

Forgetting
the question is
manufactured,
make believe.

tidy

I wish,
a hint,
neatly folded guilt
keeps things tidy
for all the rest.

No one needs to
suffer the wrinkled
pile of your conscience.

Straight rows,
stout stacks,
get the work done.

Put your burdens
in their places
to be put away
efficiently
until the occasion
to wear them
comes again.

Godot

Which clock?

Where?

Time will not spare
your urgent need
to avoid the dare.

When we see
the lockstep
our spirits balk,
kept collared
by the secondhand
we accept
as paramount
god concept.

Tick tock prayer.

Reverence
is your despair.

This rock,
this star,
this love affair
with the fluid flow
of the come and go.

This life,
this peace,
this human show
envisioning the Reaper
as our Godot.

pilgrims

Awake and vivid
visions of flesh
soft as the
nodding flowers
yet to be dismembered
by the zealous gardener.

Pilgrims fly over
the night garden.

Absorbing
the blackness
filling space
saved for air.
Hoarding
the energy
better to share.

Descending
to break from
the sojourn
compelling.
Carrying
blossoming
secrets for telling.

Sleepers reject
the din of mumbles
from judging lips
as dreams of
the night garden
do eclipse
counterfeit shame
so futile
disentangling
existential knots
so brutal.

feminine

This feminine failure
of mine is judged.
The irony
of the passive speaking
with such force
looks like
a disciplined queue
of concubines
prostrating
on knees,
one by one.

This charred recollection
of the rejection
wanders the landscape
with emaciated hope.
Finding survivors
of the firestorm
may prove more work
than it is worth
after they are coaxed
back to life.

Memories of self
before
scorched,
tainted,
not fit
for consumption,
remind me
of newly turned earth
after a rain.
Earth that bleeds,
indifferent of seeds,
receptive of needs,
beyond the mystical,
logistical
drive to breed.

Wide hips,
flowering lips,
coexist,
yet eclipse
the resistance
to receiving,
a portend conceiving,
a female deceiving
of all that serves her,
after
the revolutionary stir,
heretics endure.

maternal

My wanderlust
is catching up
with my hard-won
maternal instinct.
The universal giver
I so valiantly battled
has laid claim
to a sliver
of my spirit
that anchors me
against my will.
This foreign
biological drive
ties me
to beings
that thrive
despite my
thrashing core.

method

Give up
your trickster
brain for a time.

Feel.
Love.

The sand of life
in your toes.
The mud of existence
in your fingers.
The mess
with purpose.

Neatness belies
the true experience.

Your mindvoice
sings opera,
claims genius,
resolves the theory
of everything,
declares love
for more than one.

It seems madness.

They say
there is method
to the madness.
When you live it,
you know
the method
is madness.

Listen!
Your mindvoice sings.

die

I want to die with no fear.
To run arms wide,
ego prostrate,
knowing that rules are
a distraction for the distractible.

I will jump into the abyss.
With eyes open,
memories dancing,
feeling that every moment
was Illuminati incarnate.

The fire laps at my toes,
yet my peace lives
through the burn.
Such truth
will only speak
to those who discern.

From pledging allegiance
to the stage and page,
I have no time
for opponent rage.

Every breath
ecstasy opportune,
with this night I am
the new moon.

11. seize

sequel

Familiar
milky curves
punctuated
by the sun,
accessories
and sustenance,
pleasure
and angst.

Recalibrated,
sculpted,
examined,
incinerated.

The story
of the scalpel
and the microscope
is the final chapter.

Bracing for the sequel,
I will wear my skin
knowing who is inside.

Beauty is of the mind,
the body its slave.

Deliberate glancing
in every mirror
until the reflection
is correct.

net

Conjuring bright dark,
contorting shapes
into ravens stark,
each eye piercing,
looking through,
stepping into my debut,
as alter ego,
surrendering force,
resistance,
yet I stay the course.

As feeding shadows
stokes my lust
of silhouettes
made of stardust
that wander
into my moon-drenched net.
For some a climax,
for some a threat.
Those who judge
that is what they felt,
yet others choose
to simply melt
into the acceptance
and the pleasure,
a peace and bliss
beyond all measure.

Shadow craves shadow
absorbing light.
Relinquish the certainty
of black and white.

admit

It's so tasty,
I'm licking my brain fingers.

It's when teeth are gnashing
I sleep best.

Savor your mindvoice
as it drips from your hands.
Both there
in front of your face
enticing primal responses.

No one is watching
while everyone is watching
you get carried away
in the perfectly inappropriate
pleasure of your tongue
on skin.

Drown in the texture,
lapping up ideas
you would never admit.
They drip from your lips
regardless of permission granted.

Collapse to your knees.
Let go.
Your judgment
of self is
obsolete.

unframed

Slow,
lumbering
compression
of breath
and flow.
Funnel all
there is
through to
the wound
bypassing
the usual
pathways
to delight
and illumination.
Grayscale and flat
as the colors
are all used up
in earlier portraits,
this painting
will remain
unframed.

enterprise

The reverie,
it clings to me,
when I am
the dreamer
that sets it free.

Anticipating
the juicy
tastes of real
as words do not
describe but
are the meal.

Lessons of love
embody many
with pleasure
accepted by
scarcely any.

Stumbling
defiantly
in the direction
of delirium
bleeding conformity
to attain equilibrium.

Hyperventilation
in honor of pain
feeds the need
to mock entertain.

Owning the future
because of the past
makes the flow
simple,
the enterprise
outcast.

crutches

Like a
one-way
mirror,
the sensation
allows for
a peep show
observance.

Utilitarian,
unsatisfying.

Time to swallow
the second-rate,
the day-old.
Time to buy
the dented can.

Empathy is
a traveling tent
revival.
See
the convincing
tangle of obsolete
crutches?
Everyone will
get home fine
without.

If not,
there will be
a tent
down the road
tomorrow
selling a pair
that feels
almost the same.

steadfast

No appetite to heed.
No sleep you need.
Not certain if cut,
you will bleed.

As human
as the next
dear spirit,
you assure
the others:
No need to fear it.

Swallowing fire,
brimstone deflected,
the locusts are friends,
no plague infected.

Standing steadfast
against the suffering,
isolation neatly
translated comforting.

Flesh melted.
Hair burning.
After the bomb,
there is no yearning.

scribe

Redact the pain.
Examine if words
remain the same.
The static both
launches and stunts
this brain.

Phantom sensate
focused to abate
the destruction of
compulsion
to create.

Harlequin garden
plush from sweat
teases
the deep
mind vignette
is lost along
with all regret.

Yet silence
seems to reflect
the images
to follow by tesseract
which live and dance
through side effect.

At once,
whole
comes the story
whimsical,
macabre,
ecstatic,
gory.

A fortunate scribe
to channel complete
healing universal flow
replete with sustenance
for all to thrive,
allowing every passion
to come alive.

hall

Lonely is
the night black hall.
Where you walk,
no sleep will call.

No one opens
their eyes wider
than those who attempt
to solve the cipher.

In the dark
there are no clues,
except the tickling
by the muse.

Survival is
some blissful rest.
Yet not for those
by words possessed.

ringmaster

Needs too great to voice
have a vortex all their own.
The beauty of that heavy blanket can be
stained by the inconvenience of its weight.
The two mingling with all the rest of the
constellation of revolving-door responsibilities.

I walk and nod and smile
the smile of the ringmaster
not willing to expose
the crushing secrets of the circus.
Those who have paid admission
will not see their amusement spoiled.
We nod together complicit in
the commitment to not ask or tell.

Upon finding the tent dark,
the ringmaster smile fades
for lack of people to show.
The perpetual work of
the traveling itself becomes
the revolving door
with no direction or destination.

Unless the show goes on,
the pattern is incessant, monotonous.
So with the unbridled momentum
of what has always been,
tents assembled, high wires hoisted,
time to muster with a ringmaster smile.

phosphoresce

The lengths
I have
gone to
acquiring
these scars,
Romantics
will clamor
to ever etch
in the stars.

The trains
I have
conjured
in front of
which
to stand.

The death
I have
absorbed
to deceive
the sleight
of hand.

The defiance
I have
stoked
to infuriate
~~the man~~
thus far,
will only
make certain
to phosphoresce
in bell jars.

charge

Pulling
sheets apart
in the dark.
Making fireworks
and the bed.

Releasing
the charge
of electric stars.
Natural magic
goes to my head.

teeth

Pain is lonelier
in the dark.
Despite
the tossing
and turning,
it hunts.
Selling your soul
is the
logical solution.
Incessant
invisible
battering
creates accumulated
delusion.

No heroes
diving through
sugar glass
to put an end
to this mess.

Just the ominous
brooding shadow
of the savage
with yellow horns.
Only foreboding
until you are
in his arms.
Comfort comes cheap
and costs much
as teeth incise
and an expensive peace
descends.

stem

Hold that
elegant
glass of blood
by the stem.

No one will tolerate
your frightful manners.

Sip delicately.
No gulping.

Manage your intoxication
in order to be invited back.

Krista Ann Hammerbacher Haapala

familiar

The last time
I saw the moon
I was whole,
put together
in all
the right places.

Now that the moon
has disappeared
I am scrambled,
disassembled
and rearranged.

It is time
for the moon
to return
and reflect
sunlight
into this
confused,
confounding
darkness.

Illuminated
by moonlight,
I have faith
I will look
familiar.

virulent

The virulent emptiness
of the ground
never gained
shapes the spirit
into humanness chained.
Immobile,
vacant,
nothing realized.
Bitter laughter
in place of creation
idealized.
Sharing from isolation,
so needy,
leads to embodying
impostors
all greedy.
Into my own eyes
I gaze for the real.
Staring back,
a judgmental ego ideal.

devout

Radiate.
Prostrate.

The universe
makes me wait.
For my own good,
I am sure.

In my own hands,
my own cure.
With too much
flowing in,
time to
shine out.

It is in me
to be more
devout.

The practice
settles right,
I soothe
the inner fight.

Now
time
to radiate
standing
upright.

III. entwine

carnal

Sliding through secrets
into the sweetness
of you on my tongue.

Here and among
the flesh and the heat,
our desires they meet,
amplifying the hunger.

The lightning and thunder
we make while entwined,
a consensual binding,
body and mind.

Lost in the deepness
of this carnal genius
there is only now,
the touch and the sound,
base and profound.

With you,
the lost is where
I am found.

refuge

The bounce
to insanity
takes
no time
at all.

The panorama
becomes
your Love's eyes
in an instant.

Only feeling.
Only pain.
Only eyes.
Only connection.

In every
parallel universe,
I die
without his eyes.

In this
one universe,
I leave
my body
to reside
within him
as the recalibration
rages
through my cells.

Shaken so hard,
to tatters,
to fiery bits,
only conceptual
understanding
of self remains.

Reduced to elements,
where time is all, yet
does not exist, he
absorbs me, preserves
me whole, as I seek
refuge.

space

Love is where
you live in me
as I hope to in you.
To make the space
we must agree
to savor the taboo.

Infinite curves
to throw us off,
yet relentless
I persevere.
Those in the dark
will only scoff,
reacting with
amorphous fear.

When first
you seek to understand,
you sense my love so vast,
you choose
to hold my outstretched hand,
making space at last.

stranger

There was a world
when you were
a stranger to me.
I lived there
not knowing
the parallel universe
awaiting my dare.
The unknowingly lost
traveler in me
felt a magnetic tug
opposite my compass
and heeded
the instinctual change
of course.
I turned
toward the stranger
who always never
knew me.
Now
you never always
know me.
You charmed
my compass true,
stranger.
All and ever you.

home

You build
your house of cards,
tender and clever.
Be not surprised
when someone
moves in.

What is fleeting to you
may feel to another
like coming home.

Quite certain
to be requited
on the doorstep
as the knocking
echoes unheard within.

The genesis
of the inevitable toppling
in order for you
to start again.

heat

The heat
you bleed
is a language
I long to master.

Some moments
I am a prodigy.
I read the code,
conquer the cipher,
unravel the message
with just my instinct.

And yet I am often
a bewildered traveler
squinting at maps
with hieroglyphic wisdom
beyond my reach.

It occurs
eventually
that the intellectual is
a delusion of illusion
leaving only love in its wake.

infinity

You.

What feeds
your hungry brain,
but the infinity machine?

Waist-deep in love
you press on
through the resistance,
feeling it rise higher,
creeping up your ribs.

Footstep after footstep
into the viscous love.

It threatens
around your shoulders
You recognize it
will overwhelm you
after it flirts
with your chin.

At last,
it envelops
your head,
caressing your lungs
as you take
your first breath.

It always seemed
that love was
not for you,
daunting in its
gateway to infinity.

Wading in
is brave
adventure.
Submerging
is belief
you are worthy
of more.

Love.

plot

Once
she loves
she loves.

His voice is gone
until he seeks
to use it.

They try despite
bone-deep knowing
to the contrary.

She's not his kind.
His secrets bind.
Yet still the enthusiasm
to marry.

The answer is lesser than
the question unasked,
when the certainty
wickedly takes her to task.

The best hope is just
to breathe in, breathe out,
with the useful delusion
of benevolent doubt.

Your deliverance awaits
if you buy it or not.
This time you must own
you compose your own plot.

unorthodox

The expanse of you
confounds me.
I'm inside.
A tourist in your head.

The guided tour
is unavailable today,
so I bang about
touching all the paintings,
climbing all the sculptures.

My experience of you
will be unorthodox.
Orthodox would
make no sense.

expectations

You have
expectations
when you speak.

I bob, weave,
hide, seek.

I smolder, slither,
rather, dither.

You hold me roughly,
strike my cheek.

When I anticipate
your hand above,
I am all
and nothing
for your love.

eventually

It's living fully to swim so deep.

Inhale.

Dive.

Kick and submerge.

The effort burning energy and
worth every molecule spent.

Eventually...
eventually the tickle
then pressure
becomes an undeniable need.

Irresistible.

Finding breath above
when breaking the surface is
ecstasy that feeds the cycle.

When every dive is ecstasy renewed,
the deeper the dive risked.

story

Opening the pages.

Inhale deeply.

That old book smell.

There you are
in black and white
forever
a part of my story.

I breathe you in
nostalgic and grateful
for the moral
our story held.

We've turned
pages since,
chapters written.
Yet our interplay
remains
unthreatening,
instructive for those
who may follow.

Those pages
are hallowed,
not ripped out
or redacted.
Perhaps tear-stained,
the source of longing,
but those well-worn pages
are a vulnerable smile.

collided

We collided.
Both looking past
with no recognition
of the double helix
of our passion.

We hurry
to our cars
to sleep
outside of
each other's
house for
as long as
it takes.

transparent

Your eyes, they see.
And, me...I see.
Not notice or view,
but see through, into.

Often clouded to shield.
Yet the instinct to yield,
grows in its fire
in response to desire.

Oh, to see through your eyes
and reject the disguise
by accepting the bliss
and melt into a kiss.

Transparent for you,
when translucent would do.

Not ephemeral.
Perhaps meant to endure.
Sharing perceptions of truth
can tell us for sure.

tidal

Rise and fall,
you are divine
through all.
The humming
of life
is the inexplicable
urge to love,
to move to love,
to be buoyant
in the waves
of passion primal.
Accepting
the ebb and flow
of tidal instincts
in all of us,
to rise,
build,
peak,
roll
in rhythm
with our core
compelling,
surrender itself
vivid rebelling
when I open
our eyes
to watch
this unsanctified
liquid breath
feed our
infinite
rise and fall.

passage

You sleep.
I sigh.
I roll my eyes.

Breathing
the feeling
of you
inside.

Resisting
the why
of spending
time unconscious
when we are together.

I trust that
we are clever
enough to invent
our constant pleasure.
Yet a dizzying constellation
drawing into our vibration
seduces us
in the knowledge
that we fill flutes
from springs eternal.
Rarely discerning
between nocturnal
and that which lies
only in sensation,
savoring flirtation.

And our creation
of an island
where our truth plays,
an invitation-only
permanent phase,
where once you arrive,
reinventing alive, ever
to thrive.
You notice passage is
really one-way,
as the lovers of life will
choose to stay.

Krista Ann Hammerbacher Haapala

Poetry Loves You Back

Often diving into poetry and connecting to emotion can catalyze creativity. I encourage you to honor that instinct. Relinquish judgment. Banish shoulds.

I've found inspiration in the typical places: love and sex, nature and beauty, loss and triumph. Yet I don't judge myself when I am called to create when it feels unusual: reading about quantum physics, seeing the soap on the window in the car wash, making the bed, transfixed by the color of my absinthe, or a life lesson in a horror story that even Poe likely didn't intend.

If your spirit calls you to create, create.

Creation leads to growth.

You are a creator after all. The more you deny it, the more I will say it. There is wisdom in your resistance. That wisdom says there is a voice in you clamoring to be heard. Use it.

Without your disturbance, the universe is incomplete.

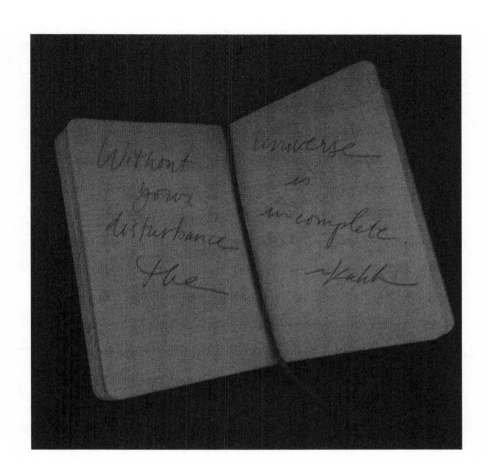

Acknowledgements with Gratitude

There are humans in my life who truly see me. They embrace my wholeness, including the heretic. My deepest bow and heartfelt hug to everyone who has supported me through Body 2.0 and the vision quest of the last two years. Love to E and Eeebs for teaching me almost everything. Mom, I wish I could hand you this book, but without you it doesn't exist. Trish, hugsandkissesloveyoukbye. Dad and Cindy, you are my unwavering source of strength and love. Love to Gramma for all that you have given me. Thank you, Roller and Jay, for our loving, cheerful connection. Meg, you will always be my roomie. Love to Fleck for never letting me forget we can be the Lizard King too. Thank you, Alison, for the space and the wisdom. Love to Tyler, Lisa, and Matt for letting me be real. Thank you, Tina, without you I'd miss the details and the fun. Thank you, Mark, for being the inspiration that you are. Love to Dave for our creative restlessness and mind meld.

And, to Brian, my Love, meum sol et stellae, we are going to do it all because we already have. You are my why.